First edition

ISBN: 9798324864798

Indendently published

Support: info@crypto-chris.com

Index

Acknowledgments

Alex Reinhardt. For his inspiration and clarity.

Hazel Moore. For helping me realise that I was meant to write this book.

Ron Palmer. For his support and encouragement

Stephan Hekkert. For the artwork.

About the author

Chris Connolly initially obtained a BSc(Hons) in optometry before pursuing further education, including an MBA, Master Practitioner of NLP, and becoming an Independent Prescribing Optometrist DipTp(IP). Shortly after completing his professional qualifications, he established his first practice, which marked the beginning of a successful career in optometry. In 2019, alongside his professional endeavours, Chris developed an interest in cryptocurrencies. Despite facing numerous scams and challenges, he persevered, learning valuable lessons along the way. Today, Chris leverages his experiences to generate sustainable income streams from blockchain technology.

Disclaimer

This content of this book is intended solely for informational and educational purposes. In particular, the information written here is not financial, commercial, investment, legal, or any type of advice. This information does not form a call to action or use of the services named. The decision to use these materials is your own. All hyperlinks lead to third-party websites, for which we are not responsible. Reference to companies or products does not imply any support from third parties. Interaction with cryptocurrencies is inevitably associated with risks and can lead to a partial or complete loss of the value of the cryptocurrencies at your disposal. We strongly recommend making informed decisions about trade, investment, or exchange and relying on professional advice. Check the services of the companies mentioned in the information provided before using their products.

Introduction

The History of money

Bartering was used as a system for trade for hundreds of years. Initially, people traded goods directly like corn for pigs or wheat for milk. This system however became inefficient due to the lack of a standard commodity values and the difficulty of finding parties that wanted to trade what you had. Simply put if you had a pair of shoes to sell and someone else had a cow to sell, the inequality prevents the trade.

Gold however, due to its scarcity, durability, and divisibility, emerged as an exchange medium. Items could be traded for predetermined weights of gold. Traders could then take their gold to Goldsmiths, who already possessed secure storage facilities to hold the gold. In time the goldsmiths started offering to hold people's gold in exchange for receipts notes. These receipts notes became accepted as a medium of payment. They promised to pay the bearer on demand the amount written on the note and became the earliest form of paper currency.

Over time, people began to recognise the convenience and safety of using these notes instead of carrying physical gold.

In time goldsmiths realised they could issue more receipts than the actual gold they held, effectively creating new money.

The goldsmiths were aware that by doing so they ran the risk that everyone could request their gold back at the same time, which would collapse their business and, cause panic driving people to remove their gold from other goldsmiths. The solution to their problem became the foundation of the banking system we have today.

In the early days monetary systems were often chaotic and prone to instability. Governments and private banks issued their own currencies, leading to frequent fluctuations in value and a lack of uniformity in monetary policy.

To address these challenges, central banks were set up to provide a centralised authority responsible for issuing currency, regulating banks, and stabilising the economy.

The origins of central banking can be traced back to the 17th century. In 1694 a Scottish banker, William Patterson proposed a £1.2m loan to the government and in return the subscribers would be incorporated as The Governor and Company of the Bank of England with banking privileges including the issue of notes. The Royal Charter was granted on 27 July 1694. On the foundation of the bank, William Patterson became a director. This was a time that saw the growth of nation-states and international trade. Over time, central banks have evolved to adapt to changing economic landscapes.

Central banks have several key functions. Firstly, the control of the money supply and interest rates to maintain price stability and economic growth. The control of bank regulation to ensure proper operational procedures and banking stability. The control of currency issuance and circulation and the prevention of counterfeiting. And to act as the last resort provider of liquidity during times of crisis to prevent systemic collapse.

In the 19th century the United States experienced frequent financial panics and banking crises. Many argued that a central bank was needed. In 1910 a meeting of the wealthiest men in the United States took place on Jekyll Island and the Federal Reserve System was born. Three years later, on 23rd December 1913 when most of the congressmen were on holiday, the Federal

Reserve Act was passed by Congress, establishing the Federal Reserve System as the nation's central bank. The Federal Reserve consists of twelve regional Reserve Banks and a Board of Governors in Washington, D.C. The establishment of the Federal Reserve System was a significant milestone in central banking history. The Federal Reserve is more powerful than any law or government. In fact, the act was written in a way that meant no government agency was allowed to investigate or oversee the Federal Reserve.

30 years and two wars later international trade had become difficult due to fluctuating exchange rates. The Bretton Woods Agreement was a post World War II agreement, that established a system of fixed exchange rates, with currencies pegged to the US dollar, which was in turn pegged to gold. Under this system, the US dollar became the primary reserve currency for most of the countries in the world, and their central banks held reserves of dollars to maintain the stability in their own currencies.

In addition, the International Monetary System was set up as an international overseer and to provide loans and assistance to countries facing balance of payments crises.

Despite its initial success, the Bretton Woods Agreement faced several challenges. Fixed exchange rates led to persistent trade imbalances, as countries with deficits or surpluses struggled to adjust their currencies. The United States experienced inflationary pressures and there were concerns about the overvaluation of the US dollar. Speculative attacks on currencies, exposed vulnerabilities in the fixed exchange rate system.

In 1971 President Richard Nixon effectively ended the Bretton Woods Agreement by suspending the link between the US dollar and gold by returning to floating exchange rates. Making the US Dollar a Fiat Currency ie a currency that is backed by nothing.

From the Latin for "let it be done," the word fiat is a binding edict issued by a person in command. Or in other words its money because the central banks say it is money.

Since World War II the US dollar has been the reserve currency of the world. This means that all central banks hold US dollars. Since 1971 however, they have been backed by a US dollar which is backed by nothing, which in turn makes all currencies Fiat as well.

This also means that of all the world's reserves and currencies are linked to and controlled by the monetary policy of the US Federal Reserve (an organisation run by a handful of the worlds richest people, with no oversight and no mechanism for investigation).

Today every country except Cuba, North Korea and Iran has a central bank. The European Union even has the European Central Bank. All the world's central banks follow the single monetary policy of US Federal Reserve.

One of the problems with this, is that when the Federal Reserve decides to print more money it dilutes the value of the reserves held by all countries. This has resulted in some countries selling off some of their dollar reserves and buying gold.

So where does money come from?
If a government needs more money than they can raise through taxation they approach their Central Bank. The Central Bank lends the government the

money and the government then issue a bond and gives it to the Central Bank. A government bond is issued to support public spending. It generally includes a commitment to pay interest, and to repay the face value on the maturity date.

The Central Bank then transfers the money to the government. So where did the Central Bank get the money from? To answer that question let us look at the word Fiat again. It comes from the Latin for "let it be done" it is a binding order issued by a person in authority. So, the banker accesses a computer, types in the amount and that amount becomes money because they said it was money and they have the authority to do so.

You and I need to have funds in our bank account to make a payment. The Central Banks just create new money to make payments. When you borrow money to buy a house new money is created on a computer and you must pay interest on it.

It is estimated that 97% of all money is digital on a computer and just 3% is the cash in our pockets. Creating new money like this dilutes the money that already exists. This means the money becomes less valuable in time and things will cost more. A system that is built on an ever-increasing supply of money is called an Inflationary System. The value of people savings reduces and the cost-of-living increases.

The Federal Reserve wanted to stimulate the economy after the DotCom bubble burst at the end of the 1990's. They reduced interest rates to 1% to stimulate house purchases. They created new money for people to take on mortgages. Unfortunately, thousands of people with poor credit scores were taking on interest only mortgages (referred to as Subprime in the USA). Then, in September 2008, US bank Lehman Brothers filed for bankruptcy and the global financial system went into meltdown.

The financial system that the Central Banks have led us into is a debt-based economy. If everyone were to repay their debt there would be no interest earned and the system would collapse.

The interesting thing is that it doesn't have to be that way. Many people are moving away from the debt-based economy into cryptocurrency economies. Like all innovations, cryptocurrencies have gone through the three stages of acceptance.

1. **Ridicule.** In the early years after Bitcoin launched people laughed, they said it would never catch on. They said it wasn't real money, and it had nothing behind it. Other coins followed and were hit with the same treatment.

2. **Violently Opposed.** As cryptocurrencies gain traction, governments enacted legislation in an attempt to curb their influence, perceiving these disruptors as a significant threat to the existing system. In the UK, recent legislation introduced in the last quarter of 2023, severely restricts payments for buying digital currencies, reflecting a proactive response to this ongoing paradigm shift. The anti-fraud departments of banks are blocking transactions and access to bank accounts if you try to purchase cryptocurrency. They do this in order to "protect you".

3. **Self evident.** Recognising the unsustainable nature of the current financial structure, authorities, driven by the fear of losing control, are developing their own programmable digital CBDCs (Central Bank Digital Currencies) These

government-issued currencies aim to assert control over your spending and reclaim authority.

Chapter 1

What are Cryptocurrencies?

Cryptocurrencies also known as Digital Currencies are electronic currencies that do not have any physical coins or notes. In 2009 Bitcoin was introduced by an unknown group or individual using the name Satoshi Nakamoto. It's first recorded price came in 2010 when a user traded 10,000 bitcoins for two pizzas, which set the value of one Bitcoin at around $0.003. From there Bitcoin's price saw dramatic fluctuations, experiencing periods of rapid growth and sharp declines. By 2011 the price had risen to around $1, and by 2017, it soared to nearly $20,000. Despite subsequent fluctuations Bitcoin's value has generally trended upwards over the years, reflecting its growing adoption and recognition as a store of value and an investment asset. At the time of writing in 2024, Bitcoin's price was over $65,000.

Bitcoin operates on a decentralised network of computers called the blockchain, which is a digital ledger like a public record book, but it is stored on many computers all over the internet. This ledger does not belong to any single person or organisation, instead, it is maintained by a network of users.

The blockchain consists of blocks which are just like pages in a book. Each block contains a list of transactions or data which are verified by network nodes. These blocks are linked together in a chronological order, forming a chain. Once a block is added and confirmed it is immutable which means it cannot be amended or deleted. This provides a tamper-resistant record of transactions, enhancing security and transparency. Cryptography is used to secure transactions and control the creation of new blocks. Public and private keys (alphanumeric strings of at least 32 characters) are used to authenticate transactions and provide ownership of digital assets. Every participant can see the entire history of transactions on the blockchain.

The original blockchains had single uses. The Bitcoin blockchain was only for bitcoin and the Litecoin blockchain is only for Litecoin.

Digital currencies are valued by the market forces of supply and demand. There are no physical assets under pinning most of these currencies, which, in reality is the same as Fiat currencies. They are decentralised which means they are not controlled or overseen by any authority just like the US Federal Reserve. The difference is that with digital currencies many participants (nodes) validate and record transactions.

Since the launch of Bitcoin in 2009 over 20,000 other digital currencies (collectively referred to as Altcoins) have emerged. Each has its own unique features and purposes.

Some digital currencies, like Ethereum and Ultima, use a new generation of blockchains called smart blockchain. These blockchains can support thousands of projects and have built-in programming languages that allow developers to create smart (self-executing) contracts with the terms of the agreement written into the code. They also form the foundation of decentralised applications (DApps) encompassing various sectors, from (DeFi) decentralised finance and (DeXs) decentralised exchanges to gaming and social networking. Their potential to revolutionise industries and reshape the internet landscape makes DApps a focal point of innovation in the digital era.

Other digital currencies, such as Ripple (XRP), Litecoin (LTC), and Cardano (ADA), offer alternative approaches to blockchain technology and have gained traction for their respective uses.

In addition to standalone digital currencies, there has been a rise in the popularity of stablecoins, which are digital currencies pegged to the value Fiat currencies like the US dollar or commodities like gold or silver. Stablecoins like Tether (USDT), USD coin (USDC) and Dai (DAI) aim to provide the stability of traditional currencies while leveraging the efficiency and security of blockchain technology.

Many digital currencies have a maximum number of coins/tokens that can ever be created. For example, Bitcoin has a maximum supply of 21 million coins, Ultima has a maximum supply of 100,000 while Ethereum has an unlimited supply. Limiting the supply of coins/tokens is an anti inflationary strategy which results in scarcity which in turn drives the value of the token upward preventing inflation.

Digital currencies are purchased from exchanges. These exchanges allow you to buy, sell or trade. They track the prices and provide historical data of how the prices have changed. Your purchase is placed in a digital wallet on the exchange. These wallets are controlled by the exchange, so it is vital that you move your cryptocurrency assets out of the exchange into your own decentralised wallet. Digital currencies are held in decentralised (noncustodial) wallets or cold wallets. Decentralised wallets provide users with complete control over their private keys, offering high levels of security and privacy. Cold wallets, such as hardware wallets offer an offline storage solution, providing an extra layer of security against online threats like hacking and malware.

Digital currencies offer several potential advantages over traditional forms of money.
They can be transferred anywhere in the world with an internet connection, enabling fast and cheap peer-to-peer, and borderless transactions without the need for banks or payment processors. Transactions often have lower fees compared to traditional financial systems, particularly for international transfers. This can make them more cost-effective for certain types of transactions.

This accessibility can be particularly beneficial for individuals in countries with limited access to traditional financial services or unstable Fiat currencies. Furthermore, digital currencies can provide greater financial privacy and security, as transactions are encrypted with a level of anonymity and privacy for users. It is worth mentioning that although anonymous, transactions can still be traced to specific addresses.

This anonymity, however, has also made digital currencies attractive to criminals for illicit activities such as money laundering and drug trafficking, leading to increased regulatory scrutiny and efforts to combat illicit use.

Security breaches and hacks of digital currencies exchanges and their wallets have also highlighted the importance of robust security measures and the implementation best practices for safeguarding digital assets. While blockchain technology itself is considered secure, vulnerabilities in software applications, human error, and malicious attacks have all posed risks to the integrity of digital currency networks.

Despite their potential benefits, digital currencies also face challenges. Significant price volatility, with the value of digital currencies fluctuating rapidly in response to market conditions and investor sentiment. Regulatory obstacles to constrain the growth of digital currencies and to make it difficult for individuals to buy them. This is happening while the central banks are quietly developing their own programmable centralised digital currencies and blockchains, which should not be confused with decentralised cryptocurrencies.

In conclusion, digital currencies represent a groundbreaking innovation in the field of finance, offering the potential to revolutionise the way we think about money and transactions. While still in its early stages, digital currencies continue to evolve and attract interest from investors, entrepreneurs, and policymakers alike, shaping the future of the global financial system.

Chapter 2

How are cryptocurrencies made?

Mining

Bitcoin comes from a process known as mining. This is a process whereby the miners use computers to figure out complicated mathematical puzzles.

Mining is the process some blockchains and some networks use to finalise transactions. It is called mining because the process also triggers the release of new coins into circulation. A lot of computing and electrical power is needed for mining. Every block has a complicated puzzle encrypted into its coding and miners use computers to figure out what the solution is. It is these high spec computers are known as nodes that consume a lot of electricity. They systematically go through every code permutation until they solve the puzzle. More powerful computers can sift through the permutations quicker than less powerful ones. The winner ie the first miner whose computer finds the solution, receives a block reward in bitcoin. It a little bit like guessing the combination of a safe. The first person to get the right answer wins the contents. As soon as a solution is found another puzzle appears for the process to continue.

In effect, mining is the process of verifying each transaction recording it on the blockchain. The process is transparent which helps eliminate double spending and makes the network hacker proof. Miners can identify cyber attacks and reject them.

Crypto miners are rewarded for their time and processing power with new coins. Bitcoin uses a halving process to reduce the number of new coins being created which in turn puts the cost of mining up. It is expected that in time, the cost to mine 1 Bitcoin will be greater than the market value of the Bitcoin.

The Bitcoin and Ethereum use a proof-of-work (PoW) system. This is a consensus system where miners compete to guess the correct solution. The first miner to find the solution broadcasts it to the network, and if validated by the other nodes, the new block is added to the blockchain, and the miner is rewarded with cryptocurrency.

The main issues with mining are the cost and the environmental impact. There is a significant outlay for the required specialist hardware and costs for the regular maintenance and repairs, and the cost of electricity due to the high power consumption. Consequently, this produces a significant environmental impact and unfavourable carbon footprint.

Staking

Staking is an alternative to mining. Instead of using computational power to validate transactions. Staking involves users actively participating in a blockchain network by holding and locking up their cryptocurrency to support the network's operations.

This mechanism plays a crucial role in the proof-of-stake (PoS) consensus algorithm, which is an alternative to the energy-intensive proof-of-work (PoW) algorithm used by cryptocurrencies like Bitcoin and Ethereum. Proof-of-stake is a consensus mechanism where validators choose to create new blocks based on the number of coins they hold and are willing to stake as collateral. It is more energy efficient than proof-of-work. Ethereum is transitioning from a PoW system to a PoS system with its Ethereum 2.0 upgrade.

In essence, staking involves depositing an amount of cryptocurrency into a digital wallet and keeping it there for a specific time period. During the time that the coins are locked they cannot be moved or traded. In return for staking their coins, participants are rewarded with additional cryptocurrency, which serves as an incentive for them to actively contribute to the network's security and stability.

One of the primary benefits of crypto staking is the opportunity to earn passive income. By staking their coins users can earn rewards in the form of newly minted cryptocurrency or transaction fees generated on the network. The value of these rewards typically depends on factors such as the amount of coins staked, the duration of the stake, and the performance of the network.

When users stake their coins, they are effectively removing them from circulation, which can create scarcity and consequently increase demand for the cryptocurrency, potentially leading to price appreciation.

Some of the issues with staking include the potential loss of trading opportunities. Staking typically requires users to lock up their funds for a certain period, during which they may not be able to access or trade their cryptocurrency. As such, users should carefully consider the risks and rewards of staking before taking part.

As blockchain technology continues to evolve, staking is likely to play an increasingly significant role in the cryptocurrency ecosystem.

Farming

Crypto farming, also known as yield farming or liquidity mining, is a practice in the cryptocurrency space where users actively take part in decentralised finance (DeFi) protocols to earn rewards or yield on their cryptocurrency holdings. It involves providing liquidity to decentralised exchanges (DEXs), lending platforms, or other DeFi protocols in exchange for incentives such as interest or trading fees.

One of the most common forms of crypto farming is liquidity mining, which involves depositing cryptocurrency into liquidity pools. Liquidity pools are smart contracts. Users who contribute liquidity to these pools are rewarded for their contribution.

Another popular form of crypto farming is yield farming, which involves using various DeFi protocols to maximise the yield or returns on cryptocurrency holdings. This can include activities such as providing liquidity to lending platforms, taking part in decentralised lending, and borrowing protocols, or staking assets in liquidity pools to earn rewards.

One of the key benefits of crypto farming is the potential to earn passive income on cryptocurrency holdings. By taking part in DeFi protocols, users can earn rewards in the form of interest, trading fees, or tokens, which can provide a steady stream of income over time.

As blockchain technology continues to evolve, farming is also likely to play an increasingly significant role in the cryptocurrency ecosystem.

However, it is important to note that crypto farming also comes with risks. DeFi protocols are still in the early stages of development and are subject to various risks such as smart contract bugs, security vulnerabilities, and regulatory uncertainty.

Additionally, the high volatility of cryptocurrency markets can also affect the value of rewards earned through crypto farming.

Splitting

Splitting refers to the process of dividing a cryptocurrency into smaller units or fractions, usually to make it more divisible and accessible to users.

Unlike Fiat currencies, which are typically divisible into smaller units (e.g. dollars and cents), some cryptocurrencies have a fixed supply with larger denominations (e.g. Bitcoin with satoshis).

Splitting allows users to transact with smaller amounts of cryptocurrency and facilitates micro-transactions, which can be essential for adoption and usability.

Cryptocurrencies can be split manually or automatically by wallet software, exchanges, or blockchain protocols, depending on the specific implementation and user preferences.

The Ultima project has taken splitting technology and smart contracts to the next level, allowing users to place Ultima into a liquidity pool and in return receive a split of the tokens released to the market each day for more than 50 years.

These concepts play crucial roles in the operation, security, and functionality of blockchain networks and decentralised ecosystems, giving many exciting opportunities for participants to contribute, earn rewards, and interact with digital assets.

Chapter 3

What are Tokenomics?

Tokenomics is the study of the mechanics that govern the supply, demand, distribution, utilisation and valuation of cryptocurrencies within the blockchain. Each cryptocurrency has a white paper that explains the purpose of a project and how it works (Appendix 1). It is a guide to its technology, features, and goals. It is designed to introduce the project to a new audience of prospective users and investors.

Token Basics

At its core, a token is a digital asset that represents a unit of value or utility on a blockchain network. Tokens can fulfil many functions, including transaction catalysts, accessing decentralised applications (DApps), participating in governance processes, and representing ownership rights to digital or physical assets. Coins are tied to certain blockchain platforms like Bitcoin. Tokens are on smart blockchains (e.g. Ethereum and Ultima). Other Tokens are issued on smart blockchain networks through token standards such as TRC-20, ERC-20 and BEP 20.

Token Supply

The coin/token supply refers to the total number of coin/tokens that exist within a blockchain ecosystem. The coin/token supply can be fixed, at the launch of the network so it cannot be changed like Bitcoin with 21 million or Ultima with 100,000 or it can be dynamic, with tokens being minted or burned based on predefined rules or algorithms like Etherium. The token supply has a significant impact on factors such as scarcity, inflation, deflation, and the overall value proposition of a cryptocurrency.

Token Distribution

Token distribution refers to the process of allocating tokens to various stakeholders within a blockchain ecosystem. This includes initial token distribution events such as token sales, airdrops, or token grants, as well as ongoing distribution mechanisms such as mining rewards, staking rewards, or token buybacks. Token distribution is crucial for ensuring a diverse and engaged community of users and stakeholders, as well as promoting the decentralisation and security of the network.

Token Utility

Token utility refers to the functions and purposes that tokens serve within a blockchain ecosystem. Tokens can have various utilities, including: -

Medium of Exchange: Tokens can be used as a means of payment for goods and services within a decentralised network.

Access and Permissions: Tokens can grant users access to specific features or functionalities within decentralised applications (DApps), such as voting rights, premium services, or exclusive content.

Staking and Governance: Tokens can be staked or locked up to participate in network consensus mechanisms (e.g., proof-of-stake) or governance processes, allowing users to influence decision-making and protocol upgrades.

Incentives and Rewards: Tokens can be distributed as rewards to users who contribute value to the network, such as miners, validators, liquidity providers, or content creators.

Asset Representation: Tokens can represent ownership rights to digital or physical assets, such as real estate, stocks, or intellectual property, through mechanisms such as tokenisation.

Token Governance

Token governance refers to the processes and mechanisms through which decisions are made within a decentralised network. Governance can be either on-chain, meaning that decisions are executed directly on the blockchain through smart contracts and voting mechanisms, or off-chain, involving community discussions, polls, and many other forms of decision-making. Token holders can have voting rights proportional to their token holdings, which allows them to participate in governance processes such as protocol upgrades, parameter adjustments, and resource allocation.

Token Incentives

Token incentives refer to the mechanisms designed to elicit desired behaviours and actions within a blockchain ecosystem. Incentives can take various forms, including: -

Mining Rewards: In proof-of-work (PoW) blockchain networks, miners are rewarded with newly minted coins for solving puzzles which result in consensus validation of transactions and securing the network.

Staking Rewards: In proof-of-stake (PoS) and delegated proof-of-stake (DPoS) blockchain networks, users are rewarded with staking rewards for locking up their tokens and participating in network consensus.

Liquidity Mining: In decentralised finance (DeFi) protocols, users are rewarded with tokens for providing liquidity to liquidity pools, facilitating trading, and ensuring market efficiency.

Governance Rewards: Users may receive rewards for participating in governance processes, such as voting on proposals, contributing to discussions, or proposing improvements to the network.

Token Economics Models

There are various token economic models that blockchain projects can adopt, each with its own set of principles and incentives. Some common token economic models include: -

Transaction Fee Model: When tokens are used as a medium of exchange within a decentralised network, transaction fees also known as gas fees are collected and distributed to network validators or stakeholders. Bitcoin uses Bitcoin for its gas fees, Tether (USDT TRC 20) uses Tron, (USDT ERC20) uses Etherium and Ultima used Smart for the gas fees.

Utility Token Model: Tokens have specific use cases or utilities within decentralised applications (DApps), such as accessing services, voting on governance proposals, or participating in decentralised finance (DeFi) protocols.

Staking and Governance Model: Tokens can be staked or locked up to participate in network consensus mechanisms or governance processes, and users are rewarded with staking rewards or governance tokens for their contributions.

Asset-backed Token Model: Tokens are backed by real-world assets such as Fiat currency, commodities, or securities, providing stability and value preservation through asset collateralisation. USDT and USDC are backed by the US dollar cash reserves or bonds.

Challenges and Considerations

While tokenomics can offer numerous benefits such as incentivising participation, promoting decentralisation and driving network growth, there are also various challenges and considerations to be aware of: -

Token Valuation: The value of tokens within a blockchain ecosystem can be highly volatile and subject to market speculation, regulatory uncertainty, and technological risks.

Token Distribution: Unequal token distribution or concentration of tokens among a small number of stakeholders can lead to centralisation and governance issues within decentralised networks.

Economic Sustainability: Ensuring a sustainable token economy requires careful balance and alignment of incentives, as well as mechanisms to prevent inflation, token dilution, or economic exploitation.

Regulatory Compliance: Are the regulatory frameworks governing cryptocurrencies and blockchain technology varying significantly across jurisdictions, posing legal and compliance challenges for token issuers and users.

Chapter 4

Halving Strategies

The halving strategy used by Bitcoin and projects like Ultima are the cornerstone of their economic models. They promote long-term sustainability and a growth in the token values. Let's compare and contrast both strategies.

Bitcoin runs on a deflationary monetary policy, characterised by regular halving events every 210,000 blocks (approximately every four years). The halvings reduce the rate at which new Bitcoins are generated, thus affecting the coin's supply dynamics.

The Ultima project created by Alex Reinhard, uses Bitcoin's principles as a starting point then uses a distinctive approach, integrating halving into its tokenomics with a unique frequency and purpose. Ultima is a system with halvings every 5,000,000 blocks (approximately every 6 months). This more aggressive strategy is aimed at creating extreme-hyperdeflationary pressure on its token supply.

Bitcoin's halving mechanism involves reducing the reward miners receive by half. Initially set at 50 BTC per block, it reduced to 25 in 2012, 12.5 in 2016, 6.25 in 2024 (450 Bitcoins a day) and

3.12 (225 Bitcoins a day) at the next halving event in April 2028.

This reduction is designed to limit its inflation rate over time until the maximum supply cap of 21 million Bitcoins is reached. The number of Bitcoin currently circulating on the market is 19.69m (CoinMarketCap).

Ultima's halving mechanism involves reducing the number of Ultima releases from the liquidity pool by half. Initially set at 51.84 Ultima per day, it reduced to 25.92 in February 2024. The next halving event will reduce the number of Ultima released to 12.96. This reduction is designed accelerate the scarcity and boost the potential for the value of Ultima to increase over a shorter time frame. The number of Ultima currently circulating on the market is 15,339 (CoinMarketCap), including those held in wallets and 7,500 held on the blockchain by the company for marketing and promotions.

By decreasing the rate of new supply, halving events inherently introduce scarcity into the system, potentially driving up demand and, consequently, the price. This deflationary pressure aligns with Bitcoin's goal of creating a store of value akin to digital gold.

Halving events often precede periods of increased volatility in Bitcoin's price and the same has happened with Ultima.

Investors anticipate scarcity-induced price increases, leading to speculative emotionally driven activity. However, these jumps are typically followed by corrections as the market adjusts to the new supply dynamics. Understanding these market dynamics is crucial for investors and developers alike when implementing halving strategies.

The halving strategy plays a crucial role in ensuring the long-term sustainability of both Bitcoin and Ultima. By gradually decreasing the issuance of new tokens, it guards against inflationary pressures and maintains scarcity, reinforcing the digital asset's value proposition over time.

While the halving strategy is designed to benefit the ecosystem, it also poses challenges and risks.

With Bitcoin the reduction in the rewards affects miners' profitability, which has lead to centralisation as smaller miners struggle to compete. Mining costs are heading towards the point where the cost to mine a Bitcoin is almost the same as the value of the Bitcoin. The market's response to halving events can be unpredictable, leading to short-term volatility and price fluctuations.

With Ultima, participants place their Ultima in the Liquidity pool in exchange for a split or portion of the Ultima released each day for a period exceeding 50 years. The halving reduces the amount of Ultima that is received which is offset by the anticipated value increase generated by the scarcity and increasing demand.

By emulating Bitcoin and accelerating the halving strategy, Ultima seeks to establish itself as a store of value and a hedge against inflation, appealing to investors seeking long-term asset appreciation. As it rolls out it will become increasingly evident that Ultima's divergence strategy will differentiate it from the other Cryptocurrencies on the market.

Ultima's long-term stability relies on increasing demand for the innovative suite of products that Alex Reinhardt is progressively introducing to the 2.8 million community members. So far there is the DefiU platform allowing members to participate in liquidity pool splitting, the U-travel platform with discounted travel, the U-Markt with over 5 million products, the Ultima Debit card linking traditional and crypto transactions, which has high spending limits can be used in over 100 countries, the Smart Wallet that can support 15 of the top cryptocurrencies with expansion to over 1,000, the Smart Exchange and U-games.

The halving strategy employed by Bitcoin and Ultima are fundamental components of their economic models. By reducing the rate of new token issuance over time, halving events introduce scarcity into the system, bolstering the digital assets' value proposition and ensuring long-term sustainability. However, while this strategy offers numerous benefits, it also presents challenges that must be navigated by stakeholders in the ecosystem.

In contrast Ethereum operates on an inflationary staking model without halvings. 1400 new Ethereum are release each day and the total number of Ethereum is unlimited. The new coins added daily dilute the value of the existing tokens.

Chapter 5

How to earn from cryptocurrencies ?

There is only one guaranteed way to walk away from your cryptocurrency experience as a millionaire:- **Start as a multimillionaire**.

Making money from cryptocurrencies can be both exciting and challenging. While there's potential for substantial profits, it is essential to approach it with caution. The industry has risks and hazards that you need to learn to navigate.

Firstly, you need to familiarise yourself with the basics and understand the various components involved. You should become familiar with the blockchain technology, how cryptocurrencies work and the diverse types of cryptocurrency available. You need to learn about wallets, exchanges, and gas fees. You need to know about surges, trends volatility and price corrections. You need to understand liquidity and smart contracts, staking and splitting.

Trading
Day trading involves buying and selling cryptocurrencies within a single trading day to profit from short-term price fluctuations.

Swing trading involves holding cryptocurrencies for a few days or weeks to capitalise on medium-term price movements.

Arbitrage trading takes advantage of the price differences between different exchanges buying low and instantly selling high on a different exchange.

AI or trading bots are often used to execute trading strategies effectively. Experienced traders use technical analysis tools and indicators to identify entry and exit points for trades. It is important when trading to consider factors like gas fees and transaction times.

It is also important to understand that the only way you can make a trading profit of $10,000, is if others make trading losses of $10,000 and its extremely easy to be on the wrong side of that equation.

Cryptocurrency trading is not for the faint hearted and should not be undertaken by the uninformed ill-educated novice.

Investing

Invest in cryptocurrencies for the long term by buying and holding them in a secure wallet. Diversify your investment portfolio to spread risk across several cryptocurrencies. Keep your eye on market trends, news, and developments to make informed investment decisions.

Mining

Mining involves the validation and addition of transactions to a blockchain network in exchange for newly minted cryptocurrencies. The main problem is that the setup costs and running costs make it prohibitive for the smaller investors to make a profit from mining. It takes about 3 to 6 years to doubled your money mining Bitcoin as the returns are 15-30% per annum.

Staking

Staking involves holding cryptocurrencies in a wallet to support the operations of a blockchain network and earn rewards. Choose cryptocurrencies that support staking, and ensure you meet the minimum requirements for staking eligibility. Evaluate staking pools or services if you prefer a more passive approach to staking. It takes about 16 years to double your money staking Ethereum as the returns are 4-6% per annum.

Providing Liquidity
Provide liquidity to decentralised exchanges (DEXs) by depositing cryptocurrencies into liquidity pools. Earn fees and rewards based on your contribution to the liquidity pool. It takes about 6-24 months to double your money with Ultima as the returns are 30-300% per annum.

Initial Coin Offerings
Participate in ICOs and token sales to invest in new cryptocurrency projects at an early stage. Conduct thorough research on the project's white-paper, team, roadmap, and tokenomics before investing. It is important to realise that there are over 20,000 different tokens with new ones being added daily, most of which never gain any traction.

Making money from cryptocurrencies requires a combination of knowledge, strategy, and risk management. Whether you choose to trade, invest, mine, stake, provide liquidity or participate in ICOs, it is essential to conduct thorough due diligence and stay informed about market developments.

By diversifying your strategies and managing risks effectively, you can maximise your chances of success in the dynamic world of cryptocurrencies.

Continuously educate yourself about the cryptocurrency market, trading strategies, and risk management techniques. Start with small investments and gradually increase your exposure as you gain experience. Set clear investment goals, and never invest more than you can afford to lose.

Be cautious of scams and ensure the legitimacy of the project before committing funds. Use CoinMarketCap, Coin Gecko the top two analytics companies to check up on cryptocurrencies. Verification of a token will give you the comfort that it has been fully vetted and passed. Verification or lack of it should be taken into account during your due diligence process. Use Certik to check on any companies with business opportunities and smart contracts that you are considering.

Once you've found the right project done your due diligence and made a non emotional informed decision commit to your project.

One you have done so observe Alex Reinhardt's 5 golden rules for success.

Rule 1. Buy tokens at a low price, and only sell them at a high price.

Rule 2. Hold tokens for the next 3-5 years. Or until the price is x3 to x10.

Rule 3. Increase your assets monthly. To increase profit and reduce risk.

Rule 4. Never sell at a loss. Always hold on and wait for growth.

Rule 5. Never break the golden rules because of panic or urgency.

Chapter 6

Cryptocurrencies and Security

Exchanges

Cryptocurrency exchanges are platforms where users can buy, sell, and trade cryptocurrencies. Exchanges should not be used to store your cryptocurrencies. Security is paramount when choosing an exchange due to the prevalence of hacking and fraud in the cryptocurrency space.

Make sure your exchange has strict security measures in place. You must use an exchange that requires two-factor authentication (2FA), like Google Authenticator or similar. Use encryption protocols and perform regular security audits.

You should read the reviews that people have given for your potential exchanges. Investigate if it has been subject to any security breaches or regulatory compliance issues especially in your country, to avoid legal issues. Exchanges with higher liquidity will be able to process your transactions quickly with minimal price slippage. And you need to choose an exchange that supports the tokens you want to trade with.

Examples of exchanges are Binance, Coinbase, Kraken, MEXC and Crypto.com. You should always do your own investigation before choosing an exchange. CoinMarketCap is a great resource for analytics of exchanges. Appendix II has a list of the top 10 exchanges listed by CoinMarketCap.

Wallets
Cryptocurrency wallets fall into two groups, centralised and decentralised also known as custodial and non-custodial. You should always use a decentralised wallet. Many exchanges also offer wallets but like the exchanges, they are centralised. The big difference is that if an exchange or a government want to freeze your centralised wallet or prevent specific transactions, there is nothing you can do about it. Nobody other than you, has access to your decentralised wallet. It can't be frozen and transactions cannot be blocked.

Wallets are digital tools used to store, send, and receive cryptocurrencies securely. There are several types of wallets.

Software wallets are Apps or programmes stored on your pc, laptop or smartphone. Examples are Exodus, Trust Wallet, and Smart Wallet.

Hardware wallets also known as cold wallets are physical devices that can be unplugged from the internet ie offline. The advantage of such wallets is that they are very difficult to hack. The disadvantage is that your wallet could be lost or stolen. Examples are Trezor and Ledger Nano. In April 24 a product called Smart Defender was introduced which stored half of the seed keys for Smart wallets. The Smart defender provides a higher level of security than Trezor or Nano with the advantage that it is easy to use. You don't need to plug it in. it just needs to be near your smart phone.

When choosing a wallet, you need to weigh up the benefits of ease of use and the security as well as the currencies supported by each wallet.

Whenever you are sending cryptocurrencies to an application you should always send it from your exchange to your decentralised wallet and then to the application. This way the exchange does not know where you are sending your funds. If you send directly from the exchange to the application, the exchange will decide whether they want to send it to the chosen application, resulting in delays and in some cases freezing of the funds.

Best Practice

There are several things that you should do to protect your cryptocurrency from theft, loss, or unauthorised access.

Always use Two-Factor Authentication (2FA). It adds an extra layer of security by requiring a second form of verification, like a code from a mobile authenticator app. Biometrics like Face ID are also recommended.

When setting up your wallet you will be required to take a note of a 12-word phrase. These are your Private Seed Keys and they are essentially the keys to your cryptocurrency wallet. Write them down and store them securely. You should consider giving a copy in a sealed envelope to your lawyer to be kept with your will. Do not store them on any electronic device. You should also consider using the smart wallet and smart defender.

Create complex passwords for your wallets and exchange accounts and avoid reusing passwords across multiple platforms.

Be mindful of malicious phishing attempts where actors try to trick you into revealing your login credentials or private keys. Always double-check any web links and never click on suspicious ones.

Keep your wallet software, exchange accounts, and devices up to date with the latest security patches to protect against known vulnerabilities. Make sure you have your wallet app on more than one device eg smartphones and laptop. This reduces the risk of a single point of failure like losing your phone or a corrupted pc hard drive.

By following these best practices, you can significantly reduce the risk of losing your cryptocurrency holdings to security breaches or theft. Remember, the decentralised nature of cryptocurrencies means you are solely responsible for the security of your funds.

Chapter 7

Investing Pitfalls and Scams

Investing in income-earning projects can be tempting, but it is crucial to be aware of potential pitfalls.

Investors may overlook warning signs or red flags in pursuit of quick profits. It is essential to conduct thorough due diligence and research before investing in any income-earning project. It is also essential that you do not invest more than you are prepared to lose.

There are many income-earning projects in the crypto space. You need to remember that this is an area with little or no regulatory controls. Cryptocurrency markets are susceptible to manipulation, including pump-and-dump schemes and price manipulation.

Be cautious of high return projects as this generally mean substantial risk. Greed can cloud judgment when investing in income-earning projects. It is crucial to remain rational and disciplined, avoiding impulsive decisions driven by emotions. If you do not, you will expose yourself risks that could result in the loss of all of your funds. Furthermore, market volatility, technical vulnerabilities, and regulatory crackdowns can lead to substantial losses.

A common theme with these projects, is that you give your cryptocurrency to a third party with a promise of high returns, generally high short-term returns.

Some income producing projects lock your funds in for a predetermined time making it difficult to access them when needed. This can be problematic and often culminates in the opportunity shutting down just before the end of the lock in period and a total loss of your funds.

Many high-yield projects rely on unsustainable business models or unsustainable returns. Once new investors stop joining or market conditions change, these projects may collapse, leaving investors empty-handed.

Income generated from cryptocurrency investments may have legal and tax implications depending on the country you live in. Noncompliance with regulatory requirements can result in fines, penalties, or even legal action. You should ask your accountant or financial advisor for advice on this.

Over the past five years, cryptocurrency scams have evolved to an unbelievable level of sophistication. They target investors through various tactics.

Ponzi schemes continue to be a significant threat in the cryptocurrency space. These scams promise high returns on investment but use funds from new investors to pay returns to earlier investors. Eventually, the scheme collapses when there are not enough new investors to sustain payouts.

Initial Coin Offerings (ICOs) have been a breeding ground for scams. Fraudulent ICOs often promise revolutionary projects or products but fail to deliver, resulting in investors losing their funds.

In exit scams (Rug Pulls), cryptocurrency projects or platforms suddenly shut down, and their operators vanish with investors' funds. These scams are prevalent in the decentralised finance (DeFi) space, especially where projects lack clarity on who is running the project and when they operate from virtual offices.

Scammers can create fake cryptocurrency exchanges or wallets to trick users into depositing their funds. Once funds are deposited, scammers abscond with the money. These scams often use phishing techniques to steal users' credentials.

Scammers can use social engineering tactics to impersonate legitimate cryptocurrency projects, influencers, or executives. They often create fake social media accounts, fake replica websites, or email addresses and use sophisticated AI to generate believable portrayals of fake CEO presentations to deceive users into sending them cryptocurrency.

Malware and ransomware attacks targeting cryptocurrency users have become increasingly common. Hackers use malicious software to steal private keys or hold users' data hostage until a ransom is paid in cryptocurrency.

Phishing attacks involve sending deceptive emails or messages to users, directing them to fake websites or platforms designed to steal their login credentials or private keys. Cryptocurrency exchanges, wallets, and ICOs are common targets of phishing attacks.

Malicious Smart Contracts: In the DeFi space, malicious smart contracts are a growing concern. Scammers deploy smart contracts with vulnerabilities or hidden functions, allowing them to steal users' funds or manipulate decentralised applications (dApps).

These cryptocurrency scams highlight the importance of conducting thorough due diligence, verifying the legitimacy of projects, personnel, head office and company registration and filing documents. Exercise caution when investing or engaging in cryptocurrency transactions.

Additionally, users should stay informed about the latest security threats and employ robust security measures to protect their funds and personal information.

Before giving your cryptocurrency to income-earning projects, carefully assess the risks involved and decide based on facts you can verify and not emotions.

Choosing projects that have been around for over 3 years are considered less risky as most scams are gone after 6 to 18 months. Choosing projects where your funds are on a smart blockchain, and returns are paid via immutable smart contracts are also better options. Avoid lock-in periods. Verify the companies head office, and if possible, visit the head office. Look into CEOs background and experience. Look at CoinMarketCap and make sure the companies token is verified and read the tokens white paper. Look up Certik to see if the company is genuine. Certik will also help you differentiate between genuine smart contracts and malicious smart contracts.

There is no way to eliminate all the risk associated with cryptocurrencies. One massive solar flare that destroyed the worlds electronics would certainly wipe out all cryptocurrencies, but other than that such extreme circumstances, caution, self discipline, and proper due diligence should eliminate many of the risks.

Frequently Asked Questions

What is Cryptocurrency?

Crypto or Digital Currencies are electronic currencies that do not have any physical coins or notes. The first Cryptocurrency was Bitcoin and it was introduced in 2009. Since then, over 20,000 other cryptocurrencies have been launched. Collectively all cryptocurrencies other than Bitcoin are collectively referred to as Altcoins (Alternative Coins).

How do I buy and sell cryptocurrency?

Cryptocurrencies are bought and sold through exchanges. These exchanges act just like the ones you use to buy and sell your foreign currency when you go on holiday. The prices change constantly, and the exchange takes a small commission for processing the transaction.

How can I keep my cryptocurrency safe?

As soon as you buy your cryptocurrency it will be placed in a wallet in the exchange. This wallet is controlled by the exchange, and you should therefore transfer your cryptocurrency to your own decentralised wallet. A decentralised wallet is only accessible by you, and you will have a 12-word phrase or key that you need to keep safe. Further security involves a offline cold wallet like Trezor and Nano or the revolutionary Smart Defender.

Why is blockchain technology and smart contracts safer, and how does it work?

Smart Contracts are blockchain programs written to instruct the blockchain to carry out certain tasks. Some smart contracts are immutable which means once initiated they cannot be altered or amended in any way. It is also possible to renounce ownership of assets on blockchain.

What are Central Bank Digital Currencies and how do they work?

CBDCs (Central Bank Digital Currencies) are government-issued cryptocurrencies aim to assert control over spending and reclaim authority over the new era of financial systems. These are on the Central Bank's blockchain and are programmable. If the government decides to limit the number of fast-food purchases per month to three and you go to McDonald's on a fourth occasion your payment will be declined. So Governments and Central Banks will have control over what you spend your money on.

How do I report cryptocurrency transactions for tax purposes?

I am unable to give any tax advice. Each country has different tax regulations. I would recommend that you speak to your accountant or financial advisor to get advice tailored to your specific circumstances.

If I placed my money in a liquidity pool on an immutable smart contract, can I get my money back?

If you have funds in a liquidity pool on the blockchain on an immutable smart contract. You will not be able to get your money back. Usually, the terms of the contract state that you would receive compensation in return for placing your money in the pool. Having said that, in April 2024 Ultima announced that they have perfected groundbreaking technology. Their new Premium liquidity pool is programmed to link with a

Buyback Pool which utilises Smart contracts to buy back splits with funds returned in 12 monthly instalments.

Does halving mean my cryptocurrency holdings are halved?

No, halving is a process used by some cryptocurrencies to reduce the number of new coins being released to the market. Each day a predetermined number of tokens is released when a halving occurs that number is halved. The purpose of halving is to combat inflation by introducing scarcity. Bitcoin has a deflationary strategy with halvings every 4 years, Ultima has an extreme-hyperdeflation strategy with halvings every 6 months.

Are there any risks associated with cryptocurrencies?

Yes, there are several risks associated with cryptocurrencies. Firstly losing the 12 word key to your wallet or someone getting access to your key keys could result in the loss of your cryptocurrency assets. Secondly, trading without knowledge and experience is risky, due to token price volatility. Thirdly giving your funds to a third party in the expectation of high rewards is the recipe for a rug pool. There are a lot of scammers out there trying to steal your cryptocurrency. Make sure you do thorough due diligence before parting with your funds. Blockchain projects with immutable smart contracts offer a lower risk profile. Use resources like CoinMarketCap, Coin Gecko and Certik to investigate any company you are considering getting involved with.

Is there any way that I can earn money from Crypto & blockchain technology without actual trading cryptocurrencies?

Yes there are lots of opportunities to make money without trading. These include Staking, mining, initial coin offerings (ICOs), creating liquidity and splitting.

Appendix I

Bitcoin white paper
https://bitcoinwhitepaper.co/

Ethereum white paper
https://whitepaper.io/document/5/ethereun-whitepaper

Ultima white paper
https://ultima.io/documents/en/WhitePaperUT.pdf

Smart white paper
https://smartblockchain.com/documents/en/WhitePaperSB.pdf

Appendix II

Top ten exchanges listed by CoinMarketCap
April 2024

1. Binance 24h Vol $20.93 Bn
2. Coinbase 24h Vol $2.71 B
3.   Bybit 24h Vol $5.35 Bn
4. OKX 24h Vol $3.13 Bn
5. Upbit 24h Vol $2.67 Bn
6. Kraken 24h Vol $1.28 Bn
7. Kucoin 24h Vol $932.83 M
8. Gate.io 24h Vol $3.44Bn
9. HTX 24h Vol $2.49 Bn
10. Bitfinex 24h Vol $276.52 m

Glossary

Altcoins: A collective term used to refer to all cryptocurrency tokens other than Bitcoin.

Bitcoin: The first cryptocurrency. Introduced by Satoshi Nakamoto in 2009.

Blockchain: Digital Ledger. The original blockchain where linked to just one coin. The new generation of smart blockchains can host thousands of tokens

Centralised: Systems run on single servers.

Coin: The terms coin and token are often used used interchangeably. Coins are digital assets that are native to their own blockchain. They are independent and operate on their own network like Bitcoin.

Cryptocurrency: A digital currency. The terms are used interchangeably.

Decentralised: Systems that are run on a peer to peer network on the blockchain. Examples are

DeFi decentralised Finance. DeXs decentralised exchanges. DeApp decentralised Applications

Digital Currency: A cryptocurrency currency. The terms are used interchangeably.

Etherium: A token created by Vitalik Buterin.

Fiat Currency: A currency traditional with no physical assets behind it.

Satoshi Nakamoto: An unknown group or individual who introduced Bitcoin in 2009.

Smart: The brand created by Alex Reinhardt. It includes the Smart Blockchain, Smart Token, Smart Wallet and Smart Defender.

Token: The terms token and coin are often used interchangeably. Tokens are digital assets that operate on Smart Blockchains. They do not have their own dedicated blockchain and they utilise the enhanced functionality provided by smart contracts. Ethereum and Ultima are tokens.

Ultima: A token created by Alex Reinhardt.

Further Reading

1. "The Age of Cryptocurrency: How Bitcoin and Digital Money Are Challenging the Global Economic Order" by Paul Vigna and Michael J. Casey
2. "The Basics of Bitcoins and Blockchains" by Antony Lewis
3. "Discover the treasure trove of opportunities in the cryptocurrency" by John Harrison
4. "Cryptocurrency for beginners. A comprehensive guide to Bitcoin, Blockchain Technology, and the revolution in the future of money - unravelling the mysteries of digital currencies for investors" by Morgan Flatcher
5. "Cryptocurrency for beginners. Your essential guide to blockchain, investments, Bitcoin and the future of finance" by Max Davidson
6. "Easy Crypyo the basics. An adult beginner book for understanding cryptocurrency" by Sandra Easton

Printed in Great Britain
by Amazon

42590454R00050